" It's not a question of **if** the price of real estate can be influenced... it's a question of **by how much. "**

"invaluable in today's erratic real estate market"
Wealth Creator Magazine

how to
sell
your home for
more

Ray Wood

The bestselling guide to making your
next property sale a stunning success!

featuring
**more cool
ideas & hot**
seller tips

OIV

How To Sell Your Home For More

The essential guide to making your next property
sale a stunning success.

Edition 8

OV

How To Sell Your Home For More (Edition 8) Copyright Ray Wood 2012

Published by Primemedia Marketing
PO Box 1613 Noosaville DC Queensland 4566 Australia
1300 55 66 63
primemedia@bestagents.com.au

Library Cataloguing-in-publication data:

Wood, Ray
How To Sell Your Home For More
Includes index

1. Real Property – Marketing
2. Real Estate Business
3. Real Estate Finance
4. Home Selling

Set in Vectora at the art & design studios of Mediamojo, Noosaville Queensland Australia.

"….offers readers very simple strategies for selling property that can save significant amounts of money. Invaluable in today's erratic real estate market."
Wealth Creator Magazine

"We saved $100,000 by learning real estate's trade secrets. **How to Sell Your Home for More** was a guaranteed shortcut to success. Well done and many thanks."
Paul & Jo Hickman

"We have just sold a property for 1.6 million dollars. The advice and suggested guidelines in **How to Sell Your Home for More** worked perfectly for us. I'm sure no other selling method would have achieved such a great result."
Mark & Ken Morris

"**How To Sell Your Home For More** is the property seller's bible! This is the best advice for selling on the planet. That now makes three sales and three amazing results."
Dr Warren Lett

"**How to Sell Your Home for More** is every property seller's dream come true. A tip to every page. A simple, practical and easy to read manual that every property seller will benefit from. The feedback from my clients has been fantastic."
Murray McLean. Financial Planner

"I followed the steps set out in **How to Sell Your Home for More** and it seemed to have all the answers. I'm sure I achieved a result that was at least ten percent higher than I would have otherwise achieved. The book covered everything from presentation of my home to agent selection. My property sold in less than a month for a great price."
Jodie Blight

"Getting the best price for my property was extremely important to me. I only had one chance to get it right. The **How to Sell** real estate book broke everything down into simple steps. I just followed the steps to a great result."
Fraser Martin

"WOW! I had to see it for myself to believe it! **How to Sell Your Home for More** has changed the way I look at selling (and buying) real estate. In tough market conditions, the process, as explained in the book, worked brilliantly. Thanks for the best real estate experience I have ever had."
Mark Borthwick

Fast Reference Guide

OVIII

0IX

Hello, welcome and get ready to sell for more

If you're selling real estate soon or helping someone who is, you have in your hands enough information to enhance not only the selling price of your property but the overall selling experience as well.

This book is a complete and comprehensive summary of everything I have learned over more than 25 years as a real estate professional. *You're about to discover a gold mine of tips, strategies, suggestions and guidelines that any property seller can use to create a substantial financial advantage.*

For example, I discovered very early in my career that a little time taken to enhance the visual appeal of a property substantially increases the chance of the seller achieving a better selling price. In many cases the result was far in excess of the seller's wildest hopes and dreams.

I have seen this simple but potent strategy work for the sale of tiny apartments, sprawling homes and even commercial and industrial property. I'm still amazed at how effective this strategy can be but astonished more property sellers don't put it to work. I can only assume that's because they don't know the inside secrets you're about to discover.

I recently put this formula to the test in one of the most challenging and difficult real estate markets I have ever experienced using my own property as an example.

2

"I will share with you a detailed account of how I sold my property for a price more than 10% higher than I paid only a year previously in a booming seller's market."

3

My mission is to show you how you can influence the selling price of your property by using the same approach as me.

Understandably, it's easy to become overwhelmed with the size of the job in front of you but please don't be. By choosing the right real estate professional, you will receive all the help you need to make sure your property is looking great well before the first buyer walks through your door.

Your real estate professional will be able to add real value to the process and is an essential component in selling for more.   Your agent's job is to guide you through the process and provide you with skill and support in five main areas:

1. Market Research as to other comparable homes sold and currently for sale in your local area

2. Specific presentation advice and valuable contacts, such as contractors and tradespeople in your area who can assist with presale presentation items and projects

4

3. Specific marketing homeowner demographic data particular to your area to make sure you target as many potential buyers as possible

4. Working with you to build and deliver the best possible marketing strategy to help you sell for more.

5. Negotiating on your behalf to achieve the best possible outcome

I will walk you through the agent selection process so you can make an informed choice.

HotSellerTips.Com

HotSellerTips.Com is a free resource for property sellers. The site is loaded with extra presentation tips and live interviews from experts plus an easy locator to help you find your local agent. In fact, your local real estate professional can help you source everything you'll need to get your home looking great. Simply click on the Find My Agent link at HotSellerTips.com

6

Real estate is the only investment that allows us to directly influence its value

What else can we own that is essential to our needs and has the very real potential to increase in value over time? As an investment, real estate is completely unique because we can directly influence its value!

We can't influence the value of art, wine or shares. But we can with our own property and the beautiful thing is that most property sellers don't realise they have this power. The savvy, well informed property seller will quickly convert a little knowledge and effort into a better-than-average result.

No Recommended Retail

Wherever you are at the moment, look at the objects around you. Chances are everything you can see was offered for sale at a recommended retail price. Everything from the book you are reading now to the keyboard I'm using to type these words was purchased at a recommended retail price. But real estate is different.

Property is one of those rare things with no recommended retail price. I have seen very similar homes located side by side sell within weeks of each other for completely different prices. Why? Because one seller followed a proven formula and strategy that enhanced the property's perceived value while the other seller made no effort, sold for 10% less and was on the market twice as long.

The reason a well presented property is so attractive is because buyers can more easily see themselves living in the property. I call this Mentally Moving In and it's a very important strategic step in the 'sell for more' process.

8

In fact, my favorite buyer qualifying questions is, "Do you see yourself living here?" This simple question helps me establish whether the buyer is interested in the home or not. If the buyer is not interested then price is irrelevant. However, a buyer who has visualized themselves living in the property has crossed the line from 'looking' to 'owning'. As the agent, I now have something the buyer wants and things will usually develop very quickly from here.

" Property is one of those rare things with no recommended retail price. I have seen very similar homes located side by side sell for completely different prices. "

You can do it too!

This is the fifth edition of How to Sell Your Home for More and tens of thousands of property sellers have put my ideas to work with excellent results. Now you can do it too.

Having a fully proven system for helping property sellers sell for more just makes the process easier. Regardless of what your local market economy is like or where your home might be, applying these proven techniques will get you a better result.

I believe nothing happens by accident in the world of real estate. There is no luck involved. The purchase of a home for hundreds of thousands of dollars is a very carefully considered decision. Understanding how to influence a buyer to purchase your property when there are others to choose from is worthy of careful consideration. This book will give you the winning advantage.

11

4 Hot Seller Tips to keep in mind.

1. Unlike everyday commodities, there is no recommended retail price on real estate. Ultimately, the price of any property will be almost completely influenced by local supply and demand and the skill of your agent. There are however, many ways to influence the outcome to ensure the best possible result.

2. Most buyer interest occurs during the first few weeks after a property comes onto the market. This is because it's fresh news and represents what we call the peak interest period or golden window.

3. Therefore, there is really only one opportunity to 'hit' the market correctly. To maximise your chance for success, you need everything going for you. Specifically this means creating the highest quality and quantity buyer interest from day one and being fully prepared to document your sale if required. (Keep in mind, your best offer may come quite early in your selling campaign)

12

4. Good quality photos are critical to marketing success. As we live in the digital age, the content and clarity of a photo has never been so important.

Let the experts show you how

See Photo samples and helpful hints from professional real estate photographers at HotSellerTips.com

13

How To Sell For More in A Challenging Real Estate Market

My own personal case study

A change in market conditions spells danger for many home sellers. Naturally, they worry their property is worth less as the market may have fallen. But property has some very special characteristics that make it different from any other kind of investment. How a property seller chooses to exploit that difference will greatly influence their success.

If we own shares, we can instantly check to see what the actual price or value of our shares may be. Obviously, share prices change almost daily depending on demand for a particular stock. When we decide to sell our shares there is nothing we can do to make our investment more competitive in the market. A share is a share.

14

The capital markets and trading volume determine a company's share price or recommended retail price. In other words, anyone can see the listed price of a stock and make a decision to buy based on the price and its perceived value. However, with property we have many opportunities to influence our potential selling price. That's just one more reason why I believe real estate is the superior investment choice.

For many years I have helped property sellers achieve the best possible result. Each time I did this by following a proven formula to ensure the best possible financial outcome for my client, the seller.

Each result was achieved with a combination of essential presentation steps and a marketing process I developed called The Sell for More System. Getting the formula right is a little like baking bread. A little too much of this or too little of that and it won't rise.

I wanted to try my system in a challenging market just to be sure and for the first time in living memory I had the ultimate 'testing ground'.

15

Real Estate's Perfect Storm

The property selling climate for my test was challenging to say the least. Gathering economic storm clouds were dark and threatening. The stock market was in turmoil. Each night, the leading news stories painted bleak obituaries of record layoffs, blood on Wall Street and collapsing financial markets around the globe. World leaders were meeting to plan an escape from a forthcoming 'global financial collapse'.

Newspapers struck fear into the hearts of readers with headlines like "Global financial meltdown", "The Great Recession", "Worse than 1929", "Banks should be safe but who knows", "Record layoffs" and "Shock Market".

Billionaire Warren Buffet told us the economy had "fallen off a cliff" and made reference to an "economic Pearl Harbour".

16

" I wanted to try my system in a challenging market just to be sure and for the first time in living memory I had the ultimate 'testing ground'. "

Harry S Dent's latest book, *The Great Depression Ahead* had just made the New York Times Bestseller list. Obviously, the title of his book did little to inspire confidence.

There were news stories about how the sale of safes for domestic use had increased 30% so investors could keep their cash at home. They didn't trust the banks. Retirees were losing their savings by the thousands every day and there was nothing they could do.   Sales of cheap packaged food like SPAM were going through the roof.

Every time there was a glimmer of hope, something would happen to wipe away any gains from the previous trading week.

I couldn't imagine worse economic conditions to sell a property and a better climate to test my system. I looked in depth at my local market. There were literally dozens of homes in my price range on the market for sale. Some had been there for many months. Conditions were more than perfect for my test, so I started preparing my property for sale.

18

Competing

Okay. Here's the number one thing to remember when you place your property on the market:

The enemy is any other property for sale within your area and price range.

Buyers first look at an image of your property to see if they can 'see themselves' in the picture. They will then look at the features and benefits like bedrooms, bathrooms, living areas, and vehicle accommodation. They will then make a decision as to how a property suits their needs and if they should inspect.

So make sure ALL your preparation is focused on having your property compete as well as possible with other homes for sale in your area and price range. Ignore this rule at your peril.

Do-it-yourself versus Professional

If you're like me, you can hammer a nail into a wall or drill a hole when you need to but that's about it. I genuinely admire anyone who can 'fix' things and do a professional job but I consider myself wise enough to understand it's not my area of expertise. Besides I would rather be doing something I'm good at and leave that stuff to the pros.

If you have access to a handy friend or relative then don't hold back. Otherwise, get yourself a pro. Here's why; First, it will look really good and buyers notice quality work. Second, a pro can do it quickly and it's done. Yes, there's a cost but consider it a prudent investment in future profits. It's also a nice feeling to know you did everything you could to make sure your presentation was 100%.

" Tragically, I have seen how a botched DIY job can really devalue a property. We don't drill our own teeth, why would we tile our own bathroom? "

21

Your Hero Shot

This is the main marketing photo that best summarises what you are offering. In my case, my home was fairly bland. No, make that very bland! I had a nice view of the National Park but I felt the interior could use some color and life. With this in mind, I looked at the most appealing aspects to create the best possible hero shot.

22

Influence your big surfaces.

I guess it's obvious but the biggest surfaces of any home are walls, floors, ceilings and window coverings. These are the things people notice first (because they are so obvious) and the easiest to change.

I bought my home a year before I decided to conduct my test. I bought at what I consider was the absolute peak of the market. Properties coming onto the market only lasted a week or two before they were snapped up. My house was only ten years old but the carpet was a cheap nylon faded blue color and the walls were similar.

Walls

Color is very important when you're presenting a home for sale. Good presentation does NOT mean creating a strong color scheme. It's essential to put personal color preferences aside and go for broad appeal. In my experience the best results have come by using a plain or warm white right through. Be careful trimming doorways and skirting boards with a contrasting color. The great thing about white is that you will impress more people. White is an excellent background 'canvas' for the other features you will add.

My personal favorite white is called 'Chalk USA.' I usually dilute to half strength. It will give you a very classic look. You might also try 'Antique White'. Your local, paint shop or DIY store can guide you on this.

I suggest you use matt on walls. For the doors and door frames, gloss is best. Good paint stores will offer you a small sample to try. Add the sample color near the floor covering to gauge how they look together.

24

It's important to paint before you fit new carpet. First, it costs less as the painters don't need to protect the carpet so they need less time. Second, you paint to the bottom of the skirting board which will look better when you carpet and third, there is zero risk of spilling paint onto your new carpet.

"**My personal favorite white is called 'Chalk USA.' I usually dilute to half strength. It will give you a very classic look. You might also try 'Antique White'.**"

26

Floors

So up came my old carpet. Taking up old floor coverings will help you lose any stale house smells. Carpet and paint soak up smells like tobacco, strong cooking, animals and water damage. Replacing your carpet is not a cheap exercise but considering the cost against the value of your property, it's probably the best presentation investment you can make. **Never** underestimate the importance of smell when you go onto the market.

Because my home is located in a warm humid climate, about 50% of my floor area is tiled. Fortunately, the existing tiles were okay and in any case, taking them up would have been a very expensive option. So I chose paint and carpet tones that integrated with them. Then I found a big chunky rug at IKEA that was large enough to cover a good portion of the tiled area.

To replace the old carpet I chose 100% wool Sisal. It's ridged and sturdy and looks great anywhere. The ridging allows for safe use on stairways as well if needed. As for color, I ended up going with a straw or wheat color to give the right contrast. Oh, and I also got a great deal because I asked for one. (Never be afraid to ask for a deal.)

Continuity with floor coverings is a very important part of presenting your property to sell for more. Different colors and carpet grades in different rooms give an incomplete look and make a home appear smaller than it actually is. Using one color right through is simple, very easy on the eye and helps to create the impression of a larger home.   It will also help your home look amazing in marketing images.

How to see a photo of my room

If you go to HotSellerTips.com and search for an article called 'Working The Room' under the 'Great Ideas' tab you can see my finished living room.

" Never underestimate the importance of smell when you go onto the market. "

Window Furnishings

The salmon coloured vertical blinds and cheap timber venetians I inherited from the previous owner made my rooms look out of date. I chose white solar-guard roller blinds that were made to measure for each window and they looked fantastic.

The Color Splash

Okay. We have new carpet, fresh paint and fantastic looking white blinds that are not only highly practical, they really complete the picture. In one way or another I had enhanced the look of the walls, ceilings and floors of each room in the house, including two bathrooms, laundry and garage. What I needed now was what I call a 'color splash' on my big bare spaces of white walls.

This is where your Hero Shot is going to need your serious input. More than anything, you want to get noticed. You need that color burst to make your picture jump off the magazine or internet page and make your buyer say "Wow! I like the look of that home".

Years ago, I learned this trick from an artist. Anyone can make an impressive color panel if they know what to do. It's also fun! I bought some big canvases and painted them black. When the black dried I painted and rolled on different colors. The effect was great. Well I thought it looked great and I had the color splashes I needed.

"Your best weapon when going for a color splash is yellow. It jumps out at you and is easily noticed."

32

I used yellows and reds and blues and greens in different combinations. For a few hundred dollars I had color splashes ready to hang on my big blank walls. Strong primary colors work best and give your hero shot the kick it needs.

Props

To complete your hero shot, you need some interesting and eye-catching props. It's like you have created this blank canvas that needs something big and bold painted on it. Again, my friends at IKEA came to the rescue. I found a fabulous bookshelf, bedside tables, lamps and a clock, some colourful framed prints, bar stools and a vase. I used some of my favorite furniture pieces in the picture too. A high narrow chunky timber bench and Italian high stools with white moulded plastic seats completed the picture. Natural timbers always look great.

On photo day I bought a bunch of yellow sunflowers to sit on my timber table. I put my IKEA bookshelf on the back wall and filled it with colourful interesting book covers and magazines.

On a big blank white wall I painted a black square with blackboard paint with a bar of red across the top to add a color splash. Because it was near the kitchen, I started using the blackboard as a shopping and to-do list and didn't rub it off for viewing days. After the first open house I noticed children had drawn on the board as well. My agent told me they were having so much fun with it that their mother had difficulty getting them to leave at the close of the open house. I'm sure those kids helped me sell for more by telling their mother how much they liked the blackboard. Now they can draw on it anytime they like because their parents bought my house!

How to paint a blackboard wall feature

Go to HotSellerTips.com and search under the 'Great Ideas' tab for an article called: 'How to paint a blackboard wall feature'. This will give you step-by-step instructions.

"My agent told me they were having so much fun with it that their mother had difficulty getting them to leave at the close of the open house."

35

The Photo! Go for a Pro.

Make sure your agent gets a good professional photographer to take your photos. This is too important to leave to an amateur. Yes, I'm sure you have a great camera. But unless it's a Single Lens Reflex semi-pro model with an assortment of really cool lenses, UV filters and your Mac or PC is equipped with the very best post production editing software then all your set up work and effort is really for nothing.

If you're serious about selling your home for more, hire a pro! A pro not only gets you the best possible image but also gives his or her professional advice on how to 'stage' the photo to give you maximum impact.   Every week, real estate professionals in your area use their personal contacts and resources to help sellers prepare their homes for sale. Why not ask your real estate professional for a referral.   (to find your local real estate professional go to HotSellerTips.com and click Find My Agent)

How to price your property for sale

It's important not to fall for the big mistake many sellers make when trying to assess the value of their property. They look around at what else is for sale and determine a price for their own property based on the asking price of other homes. If you're going to assess the approximate value of your property (and why on earth wouldn't you?) you need to start with recent sale prices. Asking prices mean nothing. Whatever you do, don't be drawn into letting an asking price influence your opinion.   Actual sale results mean everything and will give you the best indication of value.

In my case, I called in a few agents when I had finished my preparation work. Two were around the same price but the third was confident I could achieve a sale price up to 10% higher than the other opinions. I decided to go with agent three. I genuinely believed my efforts would reward me with a better-than-market selling price and if you're going to write a book called *How to Sell your Home for More*, you need to back it up with some evidence that proves it works!

37

" Here was my big opportunity to test my formulas and selling system. My 'GO' date had arrived and I was ready to have buyers inspect my home. "

The Big Test!

Working with my agent, we decided to 'pre-launch' my listing using the internet before other traditional methods. I wanted to gauge the volume of interest. I knew the damage overpricing a property could do. A pre-launch would give me a feel for demand. Within 4 days, I had my first inspection. By the end of the first week there had been 10. By day 8 I had 2 offers from buyers that were both in excess of the value opinion I had received from other agents. By day 10 I had a contract $4,000 below my asking price. Success was bliss!

I had bought at the peak of the market and sold in what one of the local agents told me was the worst market conditions she could ever remember. Not only had I sold for more, my contract price was almost 10% higher than I had paid the year before in a booming property market.

Selling real estate in a challenging market calls for an action plan and using a proven success formula. It's easy to sell your home in a boom but selling in anything less calls for skill, knowledge and care. I proved it could be done and I believe anyone can do the same by sticking to the basic success essentials that help you sell for more.

Special tools for a tough market

In analysing the results, I would say that my presentation efforts paid off nicely. Tough selling conditions meant it was even more important to make sure my home was set up to attract as much buyer interest as possible. I was able to compete very well in a crowded market to the point I had not one but two buyers wanting to own my home. There was no luck involved.

If you're getting ready to sell, I believe it's essential to be mindful of current market conditions in your area. You can do a lot of price research yourself. Find the best real estate internet sites and see who you will be competing with. Imagine you are a buyer searching for a home in your area. Would you be inclined to call the agent about your home? If not, why not? What would it take to make your property a compelling target for buyers?

40

Also be sure to find the average days-on-market in your area. This will help you understand market conditions and give you a target to strive for.

In many cases, the major real estate portals allow us to see how many visits a property has received online. The great advantage to this is that we can measure interest instantly and interpret it easily.

I urge you to monitor your internet traffic if possible. I have no specific formula to offer on this, however you will soon know if your pricing and online marketing campaign is working. Here's how to do it:

Find out from your agent how many online visits per week (on average) you can expect for your home. Your agent will be able to give you an estimate based on daily and weekly number of visits for popular properties currently listed for sale.

" Be sure to find out the average days-on-market in your area. This will help you understand market conditions and give you a target to strive for. "

42

Not getting the buyer interest you want?

Try this troubleshooting tip after day 10 on the market. If you are receiving a below average number of daily visits for properties in your area it simply means your pricing strategy needs to be reviewed. What's happening is buyers are viewing your listing as part of a search results summary but not clicking on your property as they don't perceive it represents value and they are not going to go to the trouble to find out more.

Keep in mind, our mission is to convert visits online to visits in person. The online Interest is your starting point. In real estate we call this conversion. We work hard to convert our online buyer leads to inspections or attendance at an open house by a genuine buyer. The variations of your market will come into play here. Every market is different but the basic essentials apply everywhere. Buyers will want to know more about a property they see and like as long as they perceive they can afford it. Typically, the **price point** versus **perceived value**

43

is a prospective buyer's primary reason for not further considering a property.

The concept of price to perception is universal. Buyers will want to know more about a property they see and like as long as they perceive it represents reasonable value and they can afford it. If your price is off their radar, it doesn't matter how great your property looks, it won't convert them to request a physical visit.

Below average to average online visits should yield more inspections and a limited chance of offers.

I love the way an increase in visits to your online marketing instantly results in more inspections. It's a direct correlation that can't be denied. However, if you're able to establish your property is receiving more visits but the number is still below average for homes in your area, you still have a pricing issue. This doesn't necessarily mean you need to do anything immediately but be mindful of the Golden Window you have for marketing.

44

Average plus online visits should yield more inspections, potential competing buyers and multiple offers.

I checked my number of visits after my home had been on the market for 3 days. I was averaging over 75 visits a day when the average in my area was 20. I knew I had a winner and my strategy was working really well. This was essential if I wanted to have buyers competing to buy my property. One buyer has nobody to compete with so there is no rush to make an offer. On the other hand, two or more buyers resulting in multiple offers are the dream of every seller. An above average number of visits told me my price was okay and my images and descriptive copy were doing their job.

45

"Keep in mind, our mission is to convert visits online to visits in person."

4 Hot Seller Tips when completing your selling checklist.

1 Are you ready to go to market? Decide your GO date. This is the day buyers will first look at your property. As the owner of the property, it's a date of your choosing. When can you be ready?

2 What needs to happen before buyers visit? You may be ready to go today or need a week or two to get things set up. Draw up a specific To-Do-List of tasks required to be completed before buyers come through. Taking a little time to consider what needs to be done will help you and your agent choose your GO date. (See pages 141 & 142 or download your Pre-Sale Checklist at HotSellerTips.com)

3 Documentation. The transfer of ownership of any real estate calls for knowledgeable and deliberate adherence to the legal process. Ask your agent what you need and take some time to learn about the process. How long will it take to get everything organised?

4 Appoint your agent. Selecting the best agent at the start of the process is a logical step that will work to your advantage. Their overall responsibility is to work with you to make sure everything is done to achieve the best possible sale outcome and that you, the seller, is rewarded with a positive real estate selling experience. The best agents will not only contribute suggestions and ideas, they will have valuable contacts in place to assist where required. More about this later.

*For more great ideas and resources in your area go to **HotSellerTips.com***

48

Planning your Marketing Campaign and the GO date

The GO date is the first day you will be ready to have buyers inspect your property. Once you have estimated how long it will take you to prepare your property for sale, you will be able to determine your GO date.

Let's say for example you decide to complete a pre sale presentation checklist that includes the following items;

- Paint internally
- Repair cracked tiles in bathroom
- Clean up your yard and plant flowers in your garden
- Clear out your garage and basement

It's essential to consider each task separately and plan your attack.

Painting a home is a big job. I'm going to assume you are not a professional painter (your buyers will know if you're not) so you'll need to hire a painting company. This will mean getting estimates and establishing how long they will need to complete the job.

The same goes for the other tasks. How much set up time is required and how long will it take to complete? Notice how the above examples are all adding visual enhancement to your property. This means you won't be ready for photos until everything is done.

Simply use your calandar to estimate how long each essential presentation task is going to take then put the deadline in your diary. Your Marketing Plan needs to begin after everything is ready. This may sound obvious but many sellers often underestimate the time it takes to complete presentation tasks. This can be a problem when you find yourself committed to advertising and your property isn't 100% ready for buyers to view.   Make sure you plan your marketing attack with your agent. Prepare your strategy and schedule the best time for your ads to begin.

50

" Setting your GO date well in advance is a great way to give yourself a deadline for action. "

If I invest 5% of my property value in pre sale presentation, how much can I expect in return when I sell?

Because we are dealing with something that has no recommended retail price, there is no formula for what your pre sale investment will return when you sell. But there is something far more important at stake here that many property sellers don't fully realise: You only get one shot at 'hitting' the market correctly. Results prove time and again, a well presented property will attract more buyer interest, buyer inspections and in all likelihood, a better contract price than the home that is not well presented.

52

14 Hot Seller Tips
to guarantee a better selling price.

Okay, it's show time! Living in a home while you're on the market can be challenging. You need to be organised and plan ahead. The good news is there's a pay-off for your trouble in the form of a top market result when you sell. Do everything within your power to 'present' to the market as best you can.

The senses of sight, sound and smell all play a special role in helping you achieve the best outcome. Let's look at how you can enhance your opportunities for success in each case:

1. There is no second chance at a first impression. From the moment a buyer enters your property, a positive or negative theme will form and grow. This is of major importance when it comes to influencing a buyer's opinion. Look at your property through the buyer's eyes. How could it be better?

2. Light is essential! If you don't have enough, look for ways to create it. Can a dark wall be repainted? Can you use a brighter light globe? Can an extra lamp light up a dark corner? Can garden plants near windows be cut back to let in more light? Could a skylight be installed? Light is a seller's best friend. Use as much as you can.

3. Space is essential too! Can you minimise? Overcrowded rooms and hallways make them look smaller. Buyers love big rooms. Remember, less is more.

4. How is your street appeal? The way your property appears from the street will greatly influence buyers. Is there anything that can be done to enhance appearance?

5. A cluttered home can severely limit the quantity and quality of buyers. Clear kitchens, bathrooms and laundries of excess 'stuff'.

6. Our mission is to make your property appeal to as many buyers as we possibly can, so keep in mind that some buyers may be allergic to cats and dogs.

7. It's best that owners or occupants are not present when buyers visit. It's the home that's for sale, not the owners or occupants. If possible, stay away while buyers are looking and let them experience the property without you there. If you have faith in the agent you've appointed, then it's better to leave and let them do their job.

8. A home needs to breathe. The most subtle scent can turn a buyer off or trigger a negative impression. Unpleasant smells like cigarette smoke, or lingering cooking and food odors can all be addressed. Wherever possible, make sure your home has the opportunity to breathe. You might also think about using artificial scents or candles to add that special appeal.

9. Retail specialists have proven that certain types of music can influence buyers to stay longer. Why not use this to your advantage when you sell and have some appropriate background music ready to play when a buyer comes through. Subtle is better. Keep it positive and upbeat. Your agent may well have some suggestions.

55

10. Clean your windows inside and out. Okay, it's a big job and you might want to hire someone to help you. When you're done, you'll be impressed with how great your clean windows look. Clean windows really add that extra shine to a home and will make any property look better.

11. Make sure you get your garden and yard in shape. Many buyers are looking for outside space but not a lot of work. A pleasant, well organised green space will add value and this is often the first thing your buyer will notice from a drive by.

12. Most buyers are really looking to make a lifestyle purchase. This means your own personal effects and the way your home looks to a buyer will make a significant impression. To some extent, they may be actually buying the way you live as much as the property itself. When you go on the market, you can cater to the largest sector of buyers by keeping your home neat, simple and practical.

56

13. The color splash! With ever increasing emphasis on a quality photo, don't be afraid to use a dynamic color splash. Flowers are handy for this or it could be a glass vase filled with oranges or lemons. How about a piece of art or unique furniture? Yellow is said to be the color with most impact so why not use it. Get creative!

14. In preparing to go on the market, it's tempting to take on major projects. You need to be careful here. Establish if the time, effort and expense will influence your end result. Perhaps ask your agent before committing to major works. You need to be certain that completing a major project will add value and buyer interest.

57

How to create the 'buzz'

It's satisfying to see how a well presented home generates enhanced buyer interest.

- A home that photographs well produces much better marketing from day one. You've created a great 'look' which translates into more buyer appeal right from the start.   Whether viewed on a website, newspaper or magazine, an interesting image says "come and look me over...I may be just the place you've been searching for". This means more buyers and the potential for buyer competition.

- More buyer traffic through your open house is a good thing. It creates a buzz. A buzz happens when interested buyers notice other interested buyers. As an agent, I love this because it means I'm doing my job of creating competition and my marketing strategy is working. It places me in an excellent negotiating position because I have something the buyer wants… their next home.

58

- When the buzz begins, I know I'm even closer to helping my seller sell for more. This is where a capable real estate professional will really add value to your result. It's one thing to create buyer competition. Handling multiple buyer offers and negotiating the best possible outcome for the seller calls for skill, care and experience.

The subtle power of creative inspiration!

Okay, I've just given you all the basics. But if you're up for it, I'd like you to also consider some serious 'attention getting' for your property that will further enhance your potential to attract even more buyers.

Let's use some creative thinking and build a marketing campaign that offers a visually compelling experience. Let's get people talking by making those 'for sale' photos look amazing and boost buyer interest.

Here again, your Real Estate professional and perhaps a home staging expert can offer a whole range of brilliant presentation ideas to really push the boundaries and transform a property from just another home for sale into a marketing 'event' that builds serious momentum.

" Let's use some creative thinking and build a marketing campaign that offers your buyers a compelling visual experience. "

60

5 Hot Seller Tips to boost buyer appeal.

1. Check out furnishing departments stores and home style shops for ideas. These companies invest heavily in home stylists and designers to create a pulled together, polished 'look'. The same look can be yours for free. All you have to do is visit the store, or check out their website for creative ideas.

2. Magazines are a great source of inspiration when you're looking for style ideas. Notice how they use the impact of content and color on the cover to get your attention?

3. Look at other homes for sale on the Internet. Just keep searching until something catches your eye. A good real estate marketing image illustrates a lifestyle where buyers can 'see themselves' in the picture.

4. Your agent should be able to put you in touch with a home staging expert. At the very least you might pick up some ideas.

5. Sometimes one interesting piece of furniture can be your anchor, playing the lead role in your image. Don't be afraid to totally rearrange a room to feature one piece of interesting furniture to get the look you want.

Listen to a live interview with a staging expert

1. Go to HotSellerTips.com

2. Click on the 'Resources' tab

3. Look for '100 Tips & Ideas' and turn on your computer audio

4. Click the play button

The Golden Window
When to sell your home for more

Have you noticed a property in your area that's been for sale for some time? After a while, the For Sale sign starts to lean over which sends a message saying "I'm tired and uninteresting".

My sympathies go out to sellers who sit around hoping for the right buyer to materialise and pay their price. Constantly getting a home ready for inspections and scheduled open house viewings is a lot of work. But it gets worse.

Let me take you inside a hypothetical open house where the property has been for sale for many months. Typically, at some point during the open house, one or more buyers will ask the real estate professional "How long has this home been for sale?" The agent will tell the buyer when the home was first listed for sale. The buyer will respond; "Well that's a long time. Why is it taking so long? When do you think the sellers will meet the market?"

Chances are the buyer is completely familiar and up to date with all recent sales in the area. They will know lot size, home size, features, what was sold with the property and the selling price.

When it comes to money, buyers have a sixth sense. They can intuitively sniff out problems and will quickly shy away from a home that's been 'sitting' for too long. Typically, they think to themselves "Well, if no one else wants this place, there must be something wrong with it".

Meanwhile the poor seller is growing tired of preparing his home for buyers and is susceptible to taking a low offer out of pure frustration.

Selling within the golden window is critical to success. The golden window represents the time segment in which it's possible to sell a property at a peak price because that's also when the property is generating peak buyer interest.

Pricing for success
A competitive asking price creates buyer competition

A funny thing happens when a red hot buyer sees a property they like. The idea of owning the home takes over their brain and their life.

They miss appointments. They forget to eat. They spend every waking hour thinking about the property and spending time there. Sounds a little like falling in love, doesn't it? In many ways, it's pushing all the same buttons.

When a buyer sees a property they like, an emotional priority takes over and they begin to plan their purchase. Their need to buy the property will only increase when they visit the open house to find any number of buyers going through the same emotions.

Have you ever noticed something walking by a store window only to find it gone when you return the next day? Suddenly your 'casual interest' rocketed to a 'have to own' scenario purely because it sold

65

and someone else wanted it too. It's like a part of us doesn't grow up from the child who only wanted to play with the toy when another child wanted it.

I recently noticed the rather speedy sale of a home for more than 10 percent over the asking price. The owners made the decision to sell the property and wanted a quick sale. The home is in a popular area close to a city and backing onto a school.

After painting and cleaning, the 1960's home in original condition was sparkling. On the advice of their agent, the owners decided to price the home competitively at $324,900. Eight days later, 12 buyers competed to produce a selling price of $365,600... More than $40,000 over the asking price.

This is not an uncommon example. In fact, regardless of market conditions, homes sell above their asking price every day because a competitive price creates buyer competition.

" Sounds a little like falling in love, doesn't it? In many ways, it's pushing all the same buttons. "

67

Gone in twenty-four hours!

There is nothing wrong with a fast sale. In fact, some of the most impressive sales happen soon after a property has come onto the market.   It helps to keep in mind that well presented, market priced property quickly attracts buyers. These properties have instant appeal in a market. Buyers will often pay a premium just to secure a property they want.

However, a quick offer may cause the seller some concern and might present itself as a red flag. The seller might think an early offer is a result of pricing the property too cheaply in the first place. They may also think it's just the first offer and there is more to come. This is where the comparable sales that were considered when the property first went onto the market play an important role. Any seller in this situation should discuss the offer with their agent and agree on the most suitable strategy.   The myth that a property needs a long time on the market to 'test' its appeal is totally false and may have serious financial consequences for the seller.

For example, on walking into your local bakery, you would probably choose freshly baked bread over the two-day-old loaf. Property is just the same. A new property, well presented and competitively priced will attract much more buyer interest purely because it's fresh, new and perceived to be reasonably priced. Make sure you're ready to consider serious offers from your Go Date.

Any seasoned real estate agent will tell you that the road to a contract is often littered with attractive early offers rejected by a seller, who eventually sells for a lesser price.   An attractive early offer is a quality problem.

69

Days-On-Market

Find out the average days-on-market time in your area

This is important as you need to know your Golden Window.

Let's say, for example, the average Days-On Market in your area is 65. This is the time from when the property goes onto the market to when a contract is completed. This means your Golden Window would begin from the Go Date (Day 1) and conclude on day 45. That's a month and half. It's more than enough time to catch the attention of a motivated buyer. After that, it's yesterday's news and buyers will start asking: "Why has this home been on the market for so long?", "What's wrong with it?" And "Why hasn't it sold?"

Advertising Vs Marketing
Don't tell us what it is, tell us what it does.

Here's a valuable lesson I learned that has helped my clients add thousands to their selling price. It's a simple technique that will attract more buyers every time. For the most part, property descriptions are dull, dry and boring. Each ad goes through the same descriptive ritual to look and sound just like every other ad.

So you've gone to some effort and expense to get your home looking great to impress your buyers when they arrive. Why not also put care into how you describe the home to prospective buyers? Lively, visual and interesting ad copy will help you bring more buyers to your door.

For a typical family, the decision to buy a home is part need but mostly emotion and when that all important emotional trigger kicks in, I believe a buyer gets a mental image of actually living in the home. This is where marketing starts and advertising stops.

Advertising and marketing are quite different. Advertising simply lists the facts and a price. On the other hand, marketing creates the emotional desire and a reason to look further. In other words, let's not tell your buyers what your property **is**, let's show them what it **does**. Features are one thing. However, the benefits associated with those features are another. Benefits will have greater appeal to your market every time.   Consider these examples:

Large family room becomes *'Big family space perfect for pizza parties and movies nights'*.

Close to park becomes *'Your children will love the sprawling parks and gardens only a 4 minute stroll from your front door'*.

Modern kitchen with ample seating area becomes *'Create dinner party magic in this fabulous entertainer's kitchen'*.

72

Most room or home descriptions just say what it is. However, good marketing should and can evoke emotion and desire by saying what it does for the buyer.

You can't sell a secret
Maximum buyer 'reach' and fishing where the fish are. How to make use of all available resources

Effective marketing is not unlike fishing. Any successful fisherman will tell you that rule number one is to fish where the fish are. This is where a good real estate professional can really add serious dollars to your selling price.

Knowing how to reach your buying market and how to 'present' the offer of your property to that market is central to your success. In fact, every time I see a seller trying to sell their own property, I wonder if they realise just how many buyers they are missing.

'You can't sell a secret' is a well known saying in the real estate industry. In other words, a property may be immaculate, fresh and supremely interesting but if you don't tell 'the world' you will struggle to sell for more.

You need to make sure the news that your property is for sale is reaching as many potential buyers as possible to achieve your goal of selling for more.

There are several essentials you need to consider. Effective real estate marketing creates buyer interest via 5 specific sources:

1. **The real estate professional's contact list**
2. **Outdoor visual (signs and directional signs)**
3. **The 'Open House'**
4. **Newspapers and magazines**
5. **Internet marketing**

1. The real estate professional's contact list

If you're not tapping into your agent's list of current buyers you're passing up a huge opportunity to generate extra interest in your property. Your agent is constantly attracting buyer interest from any number of homes they are selling.   There can only be one buyer for each home so it stands to reason the agent will have buyers left over. This is a valuable resource every seller should use to their advantage. Agents are constantly working with buyers to match them with the right home.

2. Outdoor visual (signs and directional signs)

When a buyer begins to consider an area in which they want to live, they start 'cruising'. I'm sure you've done this. I know I have many times. It's a great way to go shopping for your next home.

I drive around the area and follow the pointer or directional signs on corners indicating a home for sale. If I like the look of the property, I will call the number on the sign and find out the asking price and features if they're not listed on the sign.

Real estate professionals know that an inquiry from a sign normally means a good buyer ready to buy. The buyer has gone to the trouble of visiting the area and likes the property enough from the outside to call and find out more.

3. The 'Open House'

A buyer attending an open house may have either learned about the property from the real estate professional's listing or advertising or the company website. However they may also have just 'wandered through'. I regularly hear stories from buyers about how they noticed an open house, 'wandered through' and bought the house that day. In fact, this is not uncommon. There is something rather special about an open house and I would consider any security concerns you might have are far outweighed by the benefits you'll receive from open house exposure.

Buyers everywhere like an open house because they can view the property in a casual and relaxed way. You'll find plenty of open house tips and ideas at HotSellerTips.Com

76

" A skilled real estate professional knows how to create a great open house experience. "

77

4. Newspapers and Magazines

The mass circulation of a quality real estate newspaper or magazine is 'pure gold' for home sellers. The importance and impact will vary depending on your area. Be sure to seek advice from your real estate professional here.

The use of high quality color images to sell real estate in the print media is pretty common these days. This is also another reason to make sure you have that 'hero' image discussed earlier.

5. The Internet

Many real estate professionals tell me their internet marketing accounts for 80 to 90% of all buyer inquiries. These are staggering statistics but hardly surprising in a world where consumers expect information instantly. Why wait for the weekly property guide when you can search for real estate online right now?

Major industry sites remain the heavy hitters overall but this is constantly changing.

If there was only one source of the five I could use to sell a property it would be The Internet. However, that's just me. Be sure to speak with your real estate professional about internet marketing and how you can make it work for you and help you sell for more.

Likely Selling Range
Using your pricing strategy to help you sell for more.
Careful consideration of the facts will help you decide on your effective pricing strategy to sell for more.

The first thing to do is sit down with your real estate professional and look at the sale of comparable properties in your area. Other properties currently for sale may be mildly indicative of going market rates. But keep in mind that a listed 'for sale' or asking price really means little when assessing the likely selling range of your property.

Homes currently for sale in your area may be priced to sell or may never sell. The simple undisputable fact is that you can't consider the property a realistic comparable until there is a contract.

It's not unusual to consider a likely selling range of 10% from worst case to best case scenario with the likely selling price somewhere is the middle.

For example; Agent and seller may agree the home will most likely sell at a price somewhere between $500,000 and $550,000. So where you price the property with consideration to this range is important.

What's your story?
Your reason for selling is a valuable marketing tool

Sooner or later, a serious buyer will ask your agent why you are selling. A clear obvious answer will help you sell for more. An evasive or unclear response will not.

A certain thing happens to a buyer before they start offering hundreds of thousands of dollars to buy a property. They think to themselves "This is a big decision. Do I know all I need to know about this before I go ahead?"

Some sellers subscribe to the myth that telling the buyer why their home is being sold will put them in a vulnerable position. In fact, sharing the real reason for sale with a buyer is an important marketing weapon.

Once a buyer understands the seller is genuine about selling it's more likely to motivate them to make an offer before someone else does.

In fact, the clearer your agent is about communicating your reason for sale, the greater your chances for buyer competition and a sale at a higher price.

For example, when your agent tells a buyer you're selling to be closer to family, it's a real and logical reason. The buyer understands and can cross that question off their list.

An experienced real estate professional knows how important it is to manage a buyer's expectations. Just as every seller is concerned about underselling, every buyer is worried about paying too much.

81

When your agent tells a buyer you're just testing the market and don't really need to sell, the buyer may feel they could be paying over the odds as the seller is trying to make a profit. They may think they are paying too much.

However, a good buyer will be happy to compete if the home is what they are looking for. Suddenly price is less important. It becomes more about which lucky buyer will get to sign the contract. The seller has turned their reason for selling into a valuable marketing tool.

In most cases, I would encourage sellers to allow their agents to tell questioning buyers why they are selling. Any real estate professional will tell you that using your story as part of the marketing process can only help you achieve a better result. A genuine and believable story sits well with every buyer

Are you on the buyer's 'radar'?
Many property sellers are simply 'off the radar' as we say in real estate and this has everything to do with price and pricing for success.

Off The Radar simply means that your likely buyer doesn't 'pick up' your home on their buyer's 'radar' as it is priced way out of reach.

There is nothing wrong with beginning at a higher selling price however pricing your property competitively at the onset will definitely help you sell for more. This might sound contradictory but keep in mind when a property is on the market for an extended period of time, the ultimate contract price is likely to be lower than a price which could have been achieved during the golden window.

The following real life example makes for an interesting case study and is typical of what happens when your property is off the buyer's radar.

83

Before Craig and Melissa started searching for homes for sale in their area, they asked their bank how much they could borrow.

The bank needed their personal financial statements and salary history along with a credit check and completed loan application.

After processing the application, the mortgage officer approved a loan of $360,000 subject to a valuation of the purchased home. Craig and Melissa had saved $60,000 giving them a total of $420,000 to spend. They knew there would be costs of about $10,000 when they purchased so they both agreed they could afford up to $410,000.

They began online searches for homes in their price range and in their desired area. They also researched recent sales in the area and discovered homes were selling quite close to the asking price.

Because Craig and Melissa both worked six days a week, time was precious and they could really only afford to look at homes for sale in their price range. They specifically searched for homes in the range of $400,000 to $425,000. Anything over that was off their list. For the next month they looked at almost all the homes for sale in their price range. After four weeks they had a good understanding of values and exactly what they could afford.

A few weeks before Craig and Melissa started looking, Emily and Bill put their home on the market for sale. Bill had retired the year before and they planned to downsize to a single level home.

Emily and Bill interviewed three real estate professionals in their area and all three estimated the home would likely sell in the range of $410,000 to $425,000.

Naturally, Emily and Bill were very proud of their home. They loved their community. As the couple watched their property value increase over time, they continued to maintain it in tip-top condition. Bill was adamant there was a buyer out there who would fall in love with their home and the community. They both believed they would find someone who would pay their price. Besides, he and Emily were in no hurry. So why not start with a dream price?

They decided to list with an agent they knew who had kept in touch with them over time. Against the agent's advice, they listed their property at $465,000.

When their home first hit the market their agent received some calls from the For Sale sign but on hearing the price, buyers informed the agent they were not interested in viewing. By the end of week three, the agent had stopped receiving buyer calls.

At the beginning of week five on the market, the agent called a meeting to discuss results so far. She felt they were missing a golden opportunity to sell for a great price because buyer inquiry had dried up and many of the good buyers had either bought a home or crossed Emily and Bill's home off their list because of price concerns.

86

Their agent was also concerned because Emily and Bill's asking price of $465,000 was making similar homes in the area look like much better value. She explained how Emily and Bill were actually driving buyer traffic to other homes for sale. Finally, they reluctantly agreed to reduce the asking price to $447,000.

Craig and Melissa remember seeing Emily and Bill's home for sale at $465,000 and also noticed the price reduction to $447,000 some five weeks later. It was close to the school their two children attended and had fantastic street appeal. However, it was still way over their $425,000 search limit so it didn't even make it onto their weekend viewing list. It was off their radar.

However, another home that had just come onto the market at $429,000 did catch Melissa's attention and although it was slightly out of their price range, they decided to view the home at the first viewing time which was scheduled for the coming weekend.

When Craig and Melissa turned onto the street, they could see there was considerable interest around this new listing. In fact, the open house was one of the busiest they had attended. There were people in every room and the agent was swamped with buyers asking questions. Craig and Melissa asked the agent if they could inspect the home again on a different day as they were quite interested. The appointment was made for after work the following day.

Long story short, Craig and Melissa bought the home for $427,000. It was more than they wanted to spend but they quickly became emotionally attached to the property and knew that if they didn't buy it, another buyer would snap it up. It was fresh on the market and would not last long. Craig sold some shares and Melissa got a loan from her parents to make up the difference.

Meanwhile, Emily and Bill were getting tired of preparing their home for inspections each weekend only to have no buyers attend the advertised viewing times.   In more than eight weeks there had been no offers.

They began to realise the advice from their agent was accurate and agreed to another asking price reduction to $425,000 which was the top of the likely selling range estimate they had received by three agents two months earlier.

After three further weeks a buyer came through the open house and made an offer of $405,000. Emily and Bill were disappointed with the way things were turning out. The price reduction had failed to stimulate buyer interest. Plus, the one buyer they did have was making offers well below what they felt their home was worth. They counter offered at $420,000. After some negotiation, their agent signed both parties to a contract at $412,000.

Emily and Bill were annoyed the whole process had taken so long but pleased to have a result just the same. After more than three months on the market, they were exhausted and ready to move on. If ever in a similar situation, they would not wait so long to reduce their asking price.

By coincidence, Emily and Bill's buyer, Andrew, worked with Craig. After moving in, Andrew invited Craig and Melissa for dinner. Driving home that night, Craig and Melissa thought Andrew had got himself a bargain. In fact they believed Andrew's home was bigger and better than theirs and represented better value. It was close to the local school and the garden was larger.

This outcome is unfortunate but happens more often than you might think.   Sellers who remain on the market at a price well above their likely selling range face the very real prospect of selling for less.

The Digital Image
How to get the right shot
The rapid advances in technology never cease to amaze me.

Take advances in photography for example. The move to digital changed the industry almost overnight.   Suddenly, we could take a photo and instantly see it. We could then download this image onto our computer and manipulate composition, light and color. Then we could send it virtually anywhere or upload it to a website.

Consumers wasted no time embracing this new technology. What was once the domain of professional photographers is now in the hands of the public. Photo based networking websites like Facebook and Flickr could never have existed before the digital age.   High quality cameras with more megapixels have plummeted in price thanks to technological advances.   Software programs like Adobe Photoshop continue to become more user friendly.

Today, anyone with the right equipment can take great photos. A wide angle lens enhances the image without misrepresenting it. Filters will make a blue sky bluer or a green field greener.   Apply this technology to real estate and it's a match made in heaven.

With real estate marketing, the image is **everything**. A picture tells a thousand words and then some. An image will always generate more

91

interest than text. The better the image, the more interest it will create. It costs way more to advertise on television than newspapers or radio because television advertising (using moving images) outsells everything else.

So here's the thing that fascinates me; If a high quality image is so important for selling real estate, how come so many real estate professionals continue to use faded, dark and gloomy shots? I recently noticed a photo of a home for sale in my local newspaper. There were smudges on the photo and I realised they were rain drops! Whoever took the photo didn't even bother rolling down the car window on a rainy day to get the shot.

Starting out with a great photo is the one thing you can do to guarantee the best possible marketing of your home. Maybe your real estate professional works with a dedicated property photographer who can make your home look amazing. It's totally worth the effort and expense. In fact, it is the most important weapon in your marketing campaign.

" It costs way more to advertise on television than newspapers or radio because television advertising outsells everything else. "

Ask your agent to show you samples of photos they have used for recent marketing campaigns. If they are not top quality images then don't use that agent because you will be getting the same and definitely not selling for more.

Here's a fun challenge for you and your real estate professional. Decide on one particular image of your property to use as your main or 'Hero' shot for your marketing campaign.

5 Hot Seller Tips to make sure you get the best possible image of your property.

1. Use a professional photographer. You're selling something worth hundreds of thousands of dollars so don't miss the opportunity to enhance your best marketing weapon. It's just like you're dressing up to go out for a very important occasion. A good real estate photographer knows what to look for and after the shot is selected, they have the software to crop, size and enhance to ensure an accurate and attractive image for visual marketing success.

2. Look at content. What needs to be included in your photo set? Typically, your main photo will be of your property from the outside. What supporting photos are needed? Most major real estate web sites have room for multiple images. Some additional quality photos of the best rooms or maybe some interesting external shots to attract buyers.

3. What about a lifestyle image? Is your property near a park or boutique shopping area? Using lifestyle images to support the advantages of your location is a great idea. Keep in mind that buyers are looking at what a property can offer in terms of location as well as the home's basic layout, look and feel.

4. What did you see? Was there a particular image that caught your eye when you first noticed your property for sale? This concept of an image may well appeal to your buyer. Don't be afraid to capitalise on your buying experience and repeat the same message. Speak with your agent about including features you feel will appeal to buyers.

5. What's your 'Hero' shot? Before the digital age, we never really needed to worry about visual images, but now they rule! Advertisers refer to the main photo in a print campaign as the 'Hero' shot. This is the image they want to feature. The image that best summarises what they are selling. Your main or 'Hero' photo is the most attention-grabbing image you can muster.

How to find a great professional photographer in your area.

1. Go to HotSellerTips.com

2. Click on the 'Find My Agent' Tab

3. Enter your location details to make contact with a real estate professional in your area. Chances are they will be able to recommend a great real estate photographer and set up an appointment.

Consider a photo sign
Combine these two powerful marketing weapons and double your impact.

It's common knowledge within the real estate industry that a sign is one of the best marketing methods available. It targets the buyer who has gone to the trouble of driving around your area and agents know this buyer is usually ready to buy.

Why not speak with your real estate professional about using a photo sign to bring your best feature out onto the street. If your living room looks amazing then don't keep it a secret. If you have a magnificent view then why not show your buyers just how good it is.

97

How to build your marketing campaign

There is one very important, not to mention highly profitable reason to select your real estate professional **right at the beginning** of the selling process. A good agent is skilled at creating the right marketing plan for you. Ask your agent where their buyer inquiries come from. This is really important as there is no point advertising heavily in an area that produces few results.

Begin with their best method and establish how you can use it to your advantage. Let's say the agent's web listings are responsible for producing the most buyer inquiries. Look at which sites will be used and how your property will appear. Keep in mind, you need enough information to engage your buyers but not so much as to swamp them. I'm a fan of the bullet point features list. Overwhelming your buyers with excess copy will not help your chances of converting their online visit to a real life viewing. The mission is to tease. Let your images do their work.

7 Hot Seller Tips for creating a successful marketing campaign

1. Fish where the fish are. Before you commit to a marketing investment, it's best to know where your property will be featured. Consult your agent and establish which marketing methods are producing results. I like to keep a 'Pie Chart' to show my clients what is working best. This helps me direct marketing resources for maximum effect.

2. Establish your key points. Working with your agent, identify the three best features of your property. These may include position, size, features such as a pool or garage, a new renovation, or a view. Next, identify your key marketing feature and yell it from the rooftop! (Do you recall when you purchased your property? What was it that caught your attention? Chances are, the same thing will appeal to your buyer)

3. Identifying your buyer. There are no guarantees as to what type of buyer will buy your home. You can, however, attempt to target your buying demographic and make it easier for them to notice your property. For example, if you decide your key marketing feature is the fact you have four bedrooms plus a study then 'Large Family Home' might be your key marketing feature because you will be targeting a big family.

4. Back it up with a photo. Wherever possible, have your key photo support your key marketing feature headline and vice versa.   For example; let's say your key marketing feature headline is 'Chef's Own Gourmet Kitchen'. Your agent could then use a shot of the kitchen set up to create a gourmet feast. Don't be afraid to be creative. Have some fun and get noticed!

5. Don't overdo it. Probably the most common mistake most sellers and their agents make is including too much copy. Keep in mind that less is more and leave a little something for the buyers to discover when they inspect.

100

6. Let your ad do its job and generate interest. You can bet that no buyer is going to send a deposit in the mail without walking through your property. The most effective ads are clean, easy to read, easy on the eye with a nice image and a prominent call-to-action (inspection time and phone number)

7. Owner's notes.   No one knows your property as well as you and every home has its hidden features. Take a sheet a Paper and title it 'Owner's Notes'. Then, point by point list the home's hidden features. It may be the winter sun in a certain room, wonderful neighbors who pick up your paper and mail when you're away, a fabulous restaurant, coffee shop or park nearby. Give the list to your agent to type up and hand to buyers. Buyers love Owner's Notes because they are hearing from someone who has experienced the pleasure of living in the home. It's something fresh they probably won't receive from other homes they visit.

See How To create your Features List & Owner's Notes on page 139.

Using the Internet to help you sell for more
Welcome to the global market

My first internet lesson was a frustrating experience. My local library had just become 'connected' and a library staff member was offering free lessons. The only problem was that the connection was painfully slow. It took forever for a basic page to load. The librarian was frustrated too and offered me another lesson when the connection improved. He called me a few months later to tell me their connection was much better.

"Welcome to the global market" he announced to the small group. "Think of the internet as a shop but you don't need to hire staff or pay light, phone or rent. You can now sell to anybody on the planet who has an internet connection. Your challenge will be letting them know you are on the net too". I was rivited!

Within a couple of months, our first internet site was up and running. It was clunky and slow but at least we were out there. I loaded our listings onto the new major real estate site who had invested heavily in this 'risky' new technology. I remember speaking with one real estate industry heavyweight at the time who told me that this internet thing was just a passing craze and would soon 'blow over'.

I disagreed and promptly put him in the same category as the record company executive who turned down the chance to record The Beatles telling them that groups with electric guitars and drums would never take off!

At first there were very few buyer calls coming from our web marketing, then a trickle and finally, a consistent flow.

One day I received an overseas call. The buyer had seen one of our listings on the internet and wanted more information. We corresponded by phone and email. I arranged for her sister who lived locally to view the property. The inspection went well and the overseas buyer bought the property within a week. I felt something extraordinary had just happened. My market was in fact global and I had just proven it. The world had changed forever.

Today, I don't know of a real estate professional who doesn't receive at least 50% of all buyer inquiries online and in many cases it's more than 80%.

After that first internet marketing experience I became a solid advocate for online marketing and how it could help my clients. It was also a major breakthrough for buyers who struggled for easy ways to learn about new properties for sale. I love technology and using it to help people. I really like the way it can improve our lives. Applying technology to business has enormous potential and just as the telephone changed the way the real estate industry operated, the internet is repeating the process.

However, I believe it's equally important to understand the internet is an immediate or 'now' technology. The internet makes information

104

available immediately and consumers have become used to expecting instant results. This has changed our lives in so many ways. We now communicate via email. I can find a movie at my local cinema and buy my tickets online within a few minutes. I can book a hotel room or airfare just as easily. I can shop for goods and services any time I want and will go with the retailer that makes them available from my computer and it's not just me.

The planet is now one big global village and wherever you are, you have the opportunity to tell the world about your property for sale because you just never know who's out there. The economies of scale are unheard of. It costs the same to reach one person online as it does to reach millions.

Real Estate Agents

How to select the right real estate professional to help you sell for more

If the mission is to sell for more, choosing the best real estate professional is critical to success. There are many ways the right agent will add value to your result but essentially it comes down to this: You're about to begin a process that involves hundreds of thousands of dollars. You need to get it right first time and with so much at stake, I believe you will profit enormously from tapping into the knowledge, resources, experience and negotiating skills of a good real estate professional.

Here are the specific areas where your real estate pro will be able to add value:

- Market Research as to other homes sold and currently for sale

- Specific presentation advice and valuable area contractors who can assist with pre sale presentation items and projects

106

- Skillfully handling multiple offers to maximise the result

- Marketing knowledge particular to your area to ensure you target as many potential buyers as possible

- Fielding questions from buyers

- Guiding you through the negotiation process to achieve the best possible outcome

While helping the client sell for more is the main mission, sellers are also looking for a real estate solution. There are so many areas where a competent real estate professional can assist.

You will get more by helping your agent understand what you want to achieve. You're selling a valuable asset that has no recommended retail price. The more your agent knows, the more they have to work with and the greater the opportunity to influence your result.

6 things your agent should be asking you at your first appointment:

1. Why are you selling? (this is the first question your buyers will ask)

2. How did you first notice the property for sale when you bought? (This will help with marketing. Maybe your buyer will use the same process)

3. What improvements have been made to the property?

4. What do you like best about living here?

5. Are there any presentation items you need to complete before you go on the market?

6. Do you need assistance to relocate?

108

8 Hot Seller Tips for selecting your real estate professional

1. If I could go by only one thing as a property seller (and I have been several times), it would be the impression the agent made at our first meeting. Go with your intuition here. I know there may be a factor I'm not covering but your initial 'comfort rating' with the person who's going to be selling your property is vitally important. You'll be working with this person to achieve a specific outcome. Can you see yourself doing that?

2. The best agents I know will ask their potential clients the right questions at the first meeting. A good professional relationship needs to begin by addressing your agenda not the agent's. Every situation is different. You need to make sure you get the opportunity to explain what you want to achieve with the process. Yes, a sale for the best price is important but what's the overall objective? There's a reason behind every property sale. Your agent needs to understand your motivation to help you achieve your goal.

3. Being charged with the responsibility to sell something that has no recommended retail price calls for preparation, professional care and superb negotiating skills. Your agent needs to be able to work with you, to achieve the best possible result. You're looking for evidence they can do this. Buyers who want to buy your property will be looking to get the contract price as low as possible.   You need to be working with a skilled negotiator who is cool under pressure, can hold their nerve and knows what to say and how to say it.

4. Rate the experience! The big buzz in today's super competitive corporate world is all about 'the experience'. It's not so much about price or convenience or even choice. It's about the emotional experience because that's really all that's left. As consumers, we all want a great experience when we purchase a good or service. We want to walk away feeling good about what just happened. We got respect, courtesy, it was even fun! A good experience is great for business because it gets people talking.   I could probably find a more competitive insurance premium if I shopped around, but

when I call my insurance company I get a voice! Oh bliss, a voice!
No recorded options and buttons to press. They care about me and
respect me as a client. I'm someone to them. It's a small thing but
I really appreciate it. What kind of experience did you get from the
agents you interviewed? Keep in mind that buyers will be influenced
by the experience they receive from your agent.

5. Hire the best! The agents who pride themselves on getting the best
results will not necessarily be the ones who charge the lowest fees
for service. However, they will be the cheapest in the long run. Let
me explain. Again, keep in mind the price of your property is not
fixed. It can be substantially influenced up or down in true free-
market conditions. Ultimately, your sales price will be determined by
the skill of your agent to secure a buyer who commits to a contract
and pays the highest possible price. Consider your net result. The
cheapest agent is the one that can NET you the most. It pays
handsomely to hire the agent who has what it takes to maximise
your outcome with marketing and negotiating skill. The success of

your agent will have major impact on your financial health. If you were to undergo critical surgery, would you choose the cheapest surgeon or the best?

6. Use the network factor. Established and experienced professionals consistently work with a network of 'helpful' professionals. This is not something you learn in a real estate selling course. It's something that seasoned and successful operators work to their advantage. It will also work to your advantage as the seller. The best agents maintain a valuable contact network that will include a mortgage broker or banker, financial planners, property lawyers or attorneys, real estate investors, tradesmen and contractors. Find an agent who can access these incredibly valuable resources. The real estate professional's network could possibly do anything from help you source the best buyer to getting financing for a purchaser when no other lender can.

7. It's all about results. A real estate agent's reputation is all-important and a major influence in their success. The best real estate

112

professionals I know are motivated by the opportunity to produce the best results for their client, the seller. Their fee for service is something that needs to be earned. In the world of real estate, results speak for themselves. Every good agent knows that people talk. They know they will be judged by their result. Helping their client sell for more and earning a reputation for excellence is the kind of advertising that that money just can't buy.

8. A passionate and enthusiastic real estate professional working **with** you not **for** you is the best selling investment you will make.

*For more great ideas and resources in your area go to **HotSellerTips.com***

113

Identifying and eliminating marketing obstacles

I love going to shopping malls. Everything is primed and ready to create a retail experience. Shoppers are lured by polished marble floors. Windows gleam with colourful eye-catching displays. Soft music is playing. The air temperature is perfect. There is a lovely scent I can't quite identify and just like a casino, there are no clocks to tell you what the time is. Retailers are experts at creating the ultimate buying experience. This is a haven of happy shopping where we come to hunt and gather. Everything is co-ordinated for maximum effect: Color, light, sound and smell. Why should selling our home be any different? Don't we want to create a residential nirvana where buyers are impressed and motivated to own what we're offering?

Let's apply some lessons from the Mall example and eliminate some basic obstacles to impress every buyer who walks through your door. Making your agent's job easier will result in selling for more.

114

Owners and any pets (with the exception of goldfish) must not be present during a buyer viewing. It's a distraction and what marketers call a 'disconnect'. Leave your home free for buyers to wander and imagine themselves living there.

Clutter will kill your chances of selling for more. Hire a storage facility if you have to but get rid of excess 'stuff' and show your rooms off to maximum effect. Buyers love open space. Let's give them what they want. Less is more.

Be flexible with showing times. Reach an understanding with your agent when you first go on the market about likely viewing times and it will help if you can go with the flow. I have helped many sellers sell for more by showing their home to a hot buyer who gave us only a few hours notice.

Understanding the buyer's cycle

While you might be about to launch your home onto the market for the first time, keep in mind, your likely buyer has probably been looking for some time.

Buyers go through a three stage cycle.

Stage 1. Thinking about it

The first stage is often the longest for a buyer. They begin to think about buying a property and run through everything from a loan to moving house. This is often a very confusing time as there is much to consider. Stage 1 will often be triggered by the buyer seeing a home they like or just thinking 'what if...'

Stage 2. Searching

This is where things start to get interesting. The buyer will get serious about a loan as the hypothetical is moving towards the real.

116

Establishing how much can they afford to borrow and how much they already have will determine their buying range. They will begin to explore options and consider different locations.

Stage 2 is where the buyer will decide what they really want and look at trading off position against, size, style and condition. Do they want the best house in the worse street, vice versa or something in between? You know the drill.

This stage is also where the buyer will learn everything they can about values from sales in the area. They will learn that an asking price does not indicate actual value and begin to get a genuine 'feel' for values as their search area narrows.

Stage 3. And Action!

"Okay, enough researching. Let's buy something. This house hunting is eating into my life."

This is where the savvy home seller needs to be ready. You may only have been on the market for less than a week but when a Stage 3 buyer comes along, it's game on!. A Stage three buyer (or preferably two buyers who will compete against each other to buy your home) is tired of looking. The money is burning a hole in their pocket and they want it over and done with.

A Stage three buyer is super motivated but knows the market. Understanding the buyer's cycle will prepare you for that early offer that may be your best offer.

"We just need to find that right buyer"

Some property sellers subscribe to the theory that days-on-market is not important. They genuinely believe the right buyer will eventually come along and pay their price. Unfortunately, this seldom happens and the seller is usually forced to accept an offer much less than they might have achieved during the Golden Window.

118

The problem with this is that buyers are constantly researching what is for sale and making decisions to view properties that fit their criteria. This means rooms, accommodation, features, location and price.

Today's buyers are busy people. They can do their research on the net and save valuable hours each week by only inspecting properties that suit their criteria. Why would they look at a property that doesn't fit their buying criteria?

How to recover if your sale falls through

In the second week of my real estate career, my first ever sale fell through. All these years later, I remember it vividly. The contract included a clause to the effect that unless the buyer received loan approval from the bank, the contract would be null and void. Unfortunately, the buyer failed to qualify. Ouch! My first sale crashed and burned and I was devastated. I had worked so hard to negotiate the result only to have the whole thing go pear shaped.

"Welcome to Real Estate", my boss said to me. He told me to stop feeling sorry for myself, get back to work and help the seller find another buyer, which happened a few weeks later.

One of the biggest challenges any agent will face is helping their client, the seller, recover when a sale falls through. There is no guarantee the agent will be able to produce another buyer at the 'fall through' contract price, but it's only natural the seller will think to themselves: "We had this price once… we'll get it again".

A sale is not truly finalised or actual until it gets through closing or reaches settlement. (Buyer gets property and seller gets cash)

Facing the reality of an unsuccessful sale as soon as it happens is important. Expectations have been created and need to be addressed immediately. A good agent will meet with their client and explain what's happening and discuss available options. The reality is that a buyer may soon appear who may pay close to the original 'fall through' price. Both

120

agent and seller need to keep their options open and carefully consider opportunities as they come up. Sales fall through all the time. It's nobody's fault. It happens. Your key to a fast recovery is a plan to move on. Your agent will play a key role in this. They understand that not all sales proceed and will ease you through it.

Plan B. What to do if your home is not 'moving'

When a property has been on the market for an extended period of time and by extended I mean something well beyond the average selling time or days on market, one of three things will occur. The seller will:

1. Withdraw the property from sale.

2. Decide to sit it out no matter how long it takes in the hope a buyer will come along

3. Decide they have had enough and drop the price considerably to attract a buyer

121

The probable outcome of these three scenarios is unlikely to benefit the seller and it is certainly not a recipe to sell for more.

There is however a fourth option I have used many times with a high degree of success. I call it Plan B and it involves giving your marketing campaign a complete makeover and starting again.

During my career I have been asked many times by sellers to take over the marketing of their property after another agent has been unsuccessful. This calls for shaking things up a bit and making sure new buyers are finding my new listing on their radar.

The first thing I do is look at photos and how buyers are being introduced to the home. I look at how the home is being presented and will make some changes to capture a fresh image I can use in my marketing.

122

I then look at marketing copy. How is the property being described? Does the advertising say what it is or what it does? Are there any emotional attractions compelling buyers to find out more?

And finally I look at price. What else is the home competing with on the market? Where do I need to price my listing to make sure I create genuine buyer interest?

If the real estate industry has failed over time, it's in helping sellers understand just how much damage they are doing to their selling price by leaving their home on the market for a long period of time.

Yes, I acknowledge there are exceptions and hope springs eternal but in all honestly, who really wants to be on the market for months and months?

6 Hot Seller Tips
when your property fails to sell.

Okay! It's not a perfect world. Sometimes things won't go to plan. If your initial marketing campaign didn't achieve the result you hoped for, don't despair. Stay positive and confident about your prospects for success. There's every chance you're actually closer than you think. We just need to 'tweak' things a little. It's time for Plan B.

1. Your agent should have already identified the need to implement Plan B by now. However, just in case, call a meeting and find out what's going on. Why hasn't your property sold?

2. List the items that you think need addressing. Establish the following:

- What is the **average time** a property is on the market for sale in your area?

- **How many buyers** have inquired about your property?

- How many of these buyers have **had a look through** your property?

- How many of these buyers have **made an offer** on your property?

- **What feedback** is your agent receiving from buyers?

These answers will give you a snapshot of your campaign's success and help you decide what steps you need to take.

3. Here's an inside tip to find out what kind of traffic your property is attracting via the Internet: Most of the major real estate websites record the number of online visits each property has recorded over a given time. Some sites can provide advanced reporting of traffic on a day-by-day basis. If you don't know, establish with your agent which sites are carrying the listing of your property. By clicking on 'show visits' (if this feature is available on the site where your property is featured) you will be able to get a quick tally of online visits to your property.

125

4. Could it be price? If you've been advertising but getting little or no buyer interest, it means your price is too high. If you've been getting buyer inquiry but few inspections, it means your price is too high. If you've been getting buyer interest, inspections, but no offers, it means your price is too high. Any defect or shortcoming in any property can be compensated by price. Your Reinvention (Plan B) must address a shift in your pricing strategy. You need to send a fresh message to your market. Discuss it with your agent and consider your options.

5. A little research goes a long way. To prepare for a Reinvention/ Plan B meeting, I complete a poll of buyers who have inspected the property and ask these two questions. "Why didn't the property interest you?" And "At what price would you be interested?" Buyer response to these questions will provide valuable feedback to a seller looking for answers. In most cases, this feedback helped me make the necessary changes with results quickly following.

6. Time on the market will influence a sale price. Being on the market for a long period of time sends a negative message to buyers. They may believe there is something wrong with the property because it has been around for so long. When we begin to talk about large sums of money, suspicion is easily aroused. In general terms and in the vast majority of cases, the longer a property remains on the market, the lower the eventual sale price will be.

*For more great ideas and resources in your area go to **HotSellerTips.com***

127

How to sell for more and the 'Sell For More System'

Any important process or procedure follows a system. A good system is intuitive by nature and the operator is comfortable in the knowledge that following a proven repeatable process in a certain way produces a predictable result. The valuable by-product of this process is confidence.

A certain dominant fast food multi-national franchise has perfected their 'food assembly' business so well, it can hire young teenagers to run it. Their system produces a consistent, predictable and highly marketable product every time. Sporting coaches, Chefs, Manufacturers and Builders also understand this success principle. In fact, the better the system, the better the result. (Think Henry Ford's production line).

Any competent and successful business person knows that the system is the solution. Why re-invent the wheel and leave important procedure and details to chance when a tried and true process will give you the best result time after time?

128

When it comes to selling real estate, we know that things are a little harder to define. We know that emotion will play an important role in the process and the way a buyer 'feels' about a property will obviously influence how much they are prepared to pay. So while there can be no guarantees, there is the opportunity to employ proven strategies to influence the result. This book is exclusively dedicated to that goal.

The real estate industry has one of the highest personnel turnover rates of any profession. I believe this is because newcomers are often poorly chosen then poorly trained. In fact, many rookies receive little or no training, leaving property sellers at the mercy of incompetence.

The real estate industry has to accept responsibility here. Somewhere along the way, the selling process became a little fuzzy and unclear. With cyclical 'surges' of newcomers entering the industry, training and education tends to take a back seat to volume selling.

Every day, real estate agents who follow no procedure or proven success path are hired to sell a property. With little understanding or appreciation for the mechanics and principles of effective marketing, they simply list a home at a price and then nag the seller into reducing the price when they can't find a buyer. This causes any number of problems, but the overall result for the seller is usually a reduced contract selling price. Pricing strategy, days-on-market, presentation and marketing are all key ingredients to a great result but usually neglected by a non-trained or inexperienced rookie.

If I decided to sell my car tomorrow, I would go to an online market place and by comparing the asking price of similar vehicles, establish an accurate estimate of my likely selling figure. But it's much harder to do this with property. We may be able to estimate a general range but with real estate, there are so many more variables to consider. Also, it's unlikely there will be another property *exactly* the same, as each home has its variations and nuances.

130

" **It's especially important to employ a success strategy when selling real estate because the financial pain of error is likely to be substantial.** "

So we have a situation where we are selling something with no recommended retail price which is all the more reason to use a proven and reliable system to make sure we achieve the best possible result for our client. A good system reduces the risk and increases opportunities and possibilities.

The Bestagents Sell for More System focuses on three specific influencing factors that will decide the eventual sale price of every property;

1. The real estate professional
2. Presentation
3. Marketing

Each plays an important role and combines to generate the best result. The system is a process every property seller can use to reduce the risk of underselling and benefit from a better real estate experience.

132

The real estate professional

Because property sellers don't use the services of a real estate professional on a regular basis, they are unlikely to fully appreciate what a great pool of handy resources a good agent can be. Consider the list of benefits and advantages a competent and capable real estate professional can bring to the table.

- Buyers. A good professional keeps a current list of buyers and is also skilled at establishing who is a real buyer and who is just looking.

- Skilfully handling EVERY buyer enquiry is essential to success.

- Presentation ideas and advice. What works, what doesn't? What are the key features of any home and how do you feature them best?

- Professional contacts. Need a reliable tradesperson or contractor to get things repaired or replaced before a property goes on the market? Your agent is in regular contact with all kinds of professionals who can help?

133

- Where to advertise. How does a seller make sure their marketing 'reach' is effective? A real estate professional relies heavily on effective marketing to find the best buyers.

- Negotiation skills and experience. Almost every contract has its own unique set of twists and turns. A real estate professional is regularly involved in overcoming objections and negotiating on the sellers behalf.

- Documenting offers. This calls for timing, skill and the ability to overcome objections where necessary.

- Handling multiple offers. More than one buyer is every seller's dream. This calls for experience and skill.

- It's not just the sale. Many sellers need additional assistance after the sale and will benefit from their agent's advice and support.

Today's real estate professional does more than just 'sell'. Market knowledge, experience and success with proven ideas help real estate's

134

best agents create outstanding results for their clients. It's a personal mission to excel and achieve the best possible outcome regardless of conditions and obstacles. I encourage you to invest in the resources a good real estate professional can offer. You will not only sell for more, but enjoy the whole experience.

Presentation

It's probably obvious but the way a property appeals to buyers will have a direct effect on the selling price. Good presentation is central to every seller's success.

How To Sell Your Home For More is completely dedicated to advising sellers what needs to happen to make sure every property looks its best before it goes on the market.

In my experience, the best selling results ALWAYS occur when the seller works with their real estate professional to make sure presentation details are complete before marketing preparations (photography etc) begins.

Marketing

Marketing is the way a home is presented to buyers and also the way a buyer is introduced to a property. This all important introduction will often influence the end result. When a buyer is attracted to a property for sale, an inspection or viewing will follow and this is where emotional attraction plays a key role in the process. In other words, how the buyer feels about the viewing 'experience' will determine their attitude towards the home and the chance of a second viewing or even making an offer.

The Bestagents Sell For More System has been designed to help every property seller increase their chances of achieving a top market price. Naturally, it's impossible to guarantee an above average result, but taking the necessary steps to stack the odds to your advantage is definitely worthwhile.

Why not employ a proven system to help you sell for more?

In the opening chapter I shared my personal experience and how I was able to sell for more in a challenging market. I encourage every property seller to put these simple ideas to work. If you don't, you're really going to wonder about what might have been.

Only selected Bestagents real estate professionals are familiar with the features and benefits of the Sell For More System. To get connected with your local Bestagents pro go to **HotSellerTips.com** and click on Find My Agent.

137

" It's not a question of if the price of real estate can be influenced... it's a question of by how much. "

138

How to create your Owner's Notes & Features List

Many of your home's valuable features may well be 'invisible' to your buyers so take the opportunity to share the things you love about your home and create some notes and a simple list of features your agent can pass on to buyers. You just never know, that little 'gem' you didn't think was that important might be the difference between one buyer and three.

Your buyers will enjoy finding out more about what it's like to live in your home rather than just taking in the physical features. Your Owner's Notes take them beyond the purchase to experience the delights of actually living in their new home. Can I suggest a single sheet of paper with your Owner's Notes (A short narrative) on one side and a bullet point list of features on the other?

139

The best Owner's Notes tell a brief story about why you bought the home in the first place. What were the 'triggers'? Chances are, the next owner of your home will identify with similar needs. Be sure to include those community or proximity features your buyer may not know about like your favourite restaurant or the local Video store owner who is always ready with a good movie suggestion. Do you have a favourite specialty shop nearby? Where is the best coffee? What about your favourite Baker, Thai food restaurant, Pizza place, schools, gardens and parks, special events during the year or the walkway only locals know about? These are some of the benefits and features available in your community that your agent can't always be expected to know.

Bring your buyers into your world and share the added value they can't 'see' when they view your home.

140

Pre-Sale Checklist

Outside How is your Street Appeal?
Here are some checklist ideas to get your home prepared for exterior photos.

- ☐ Lawns tidy

- ☐ Garden and flower beds weeded

- ☐ Timber homes look great after a wash

- ☐ Does the garden need a 'cutback'?

- ☐ Front fence looking great. Could it use a paint?

- ☐ Letterbox looks good

- ☐ Street Number clear and obvious

- ☐ Are trees, shrubs blocking out a view of the house or view from the house?

Pre-Sale Checklist

Inside First impressions are almost impossible to reverse.
Let's enhance the viewing experience.

- ☐ Entrance looks great and creates a sense of arrival

- ☐ Rooms open and uncluttered

- ☐ Lots of light (artificial if required)

- ☐ Walls clean and looking good

- ☐ No smudges or marks on door jams near light switches

- ☐ Kitchen (the engine room of your home) is uncluttered, inviting and smells great

- ☐ Bathrooms clear, clean and smelling fresh

- ☐ Bedrooms ready to be 'shot' Cupboards and wardrobes uncluttered

- ☐ Living rooms open and light Ready for the camera to help you sell for more

Post-Sale Checklist

Getting ready to move
The devil is in the detail.

- ☐ Inform friends and family of new address and from when

Inform the following service of change or termination

- ☐ Internet service provider
- ☐ Telephone service/company
- ☐ Cable/Satellite/Pay TV company
- ☐ Gas service/company
- ☐ Electricity service/company
- ☐ Water service/company
- ☐ Bank
- ☐ City (rates/taxes adjustment)
- ☐ Local postal service

Getting ready to move (cont.)

- ☐ Newspaper delivery
- ☐ Cleaning service/company
- ☐ Gardening service
- ☐ Pool company
- ☐ Security/Alarm company
- ☐ Insurance company (do you have cover on your next property including contents?)
- ☐ Automated payments relating to your current home/address
- ☐ Medical, Optical & Dental
- ☐ School/s

Arrange for (find!) spare keys to windows, garden storage buildings, garage, basement and letterbox to be available.

As a courtesy to your new owner, assemble any warranty, or instruction information booklets for appliances or other equipment.

Post-Sale Checklist

Moving

☐ Get moving estimates

☐ Get moving/packing boxes (the moving company you select will often supply boxes in advance so you can get started)

☐ If possible, designate a room or area for packing and begin to pack and store the items you can. As you get closer to moving day, every minute saved will work to your advantage.

☐ Make sure you label each box as you pack and close.

☐ Book cleaners for AFTER your move

145

One more thing.
Creating a great real estate experience

Someone once told me the secret to business success is to find out why your clients hired you instead of your competition. This answer then becomes your marketing platform, your point of difference or unique selling proposition to include in your marketing.

So every time a property seller hired me to help them sell I would ask this question. Sometimes I had to do a little 'digging' to get to the real reason, as a question like this can often put someone on the spot.

There were always competitors who would charge a lower fee than me and many had vast resources or belonged to huge real estate groups with awesome marketing power. It was fun to compete in this environment because I could always show new clients how my system could help them achieve a better selling price. But the answer to my question never had anything to do with money.

146

"But how do you market Passion and Enthusiasm? How can you market something that people need to experience in-person to understand?"

The most common response was that I was chosen because of my passion and enthusiasm. I made sure they knew I would be doing whatever I could to achieve the best possible result and ensure a great real estate experience.

But how do you market Passion and Enthusiasm? How can you market something that people need to experience in-person to understand? I realised that until I met my potential client I would be fighting an uphill battle. I would be just the same as the other real estate professionals in my area. If I was going to help my seller's home stand out with great marketing then surely I had to do the same for myself. Showing sellers how they could add value to their property and sell for more was my answer and this book is the way I did it.

Simple and open communication is the key to achieving the best results. Offering sellers a proven formula for selling success with no strings attached is as simple and open as it gets. Tens of thousands of property sellers have put these ideas to work with great results.

148

Real estate is a people business and people do business with people they like. If you're selling real estate soon, I would encourage you to find someone who will work *with* you more than *for* you. Someone who looks at the day and says, "why not?" Someone who understands your mission. Someone with access to the best contacts and resources. Someone with the passion and enthusiasm to create a great real estate experience and someone with a plan who can help you sell for more. It's a team effort and you are going to need each other along the way.

Once a book is written, you can't change it but thanks to the Internet I can always give you updates. At HotSellerTips.com you'll find the latest and greatest ideas plus plenty of extras to give you the edge over other sellers in your area.

You'll be amazed at the difference a little creative planning and attention to detail will make to your result. Remember, luck is not a factor.

There is every chance your efforts will be rewarded with more buyers and the potential for buyers competing for your home, a faster sale and a better price.

You'll also be able to take enormous comfort in the knowledge that you did your absolute best to influence the value of your property.

I hope you have enjoyed reading my book as much as I have enjoyed writing it and that your selling campaign is a stunning success.

Ray Wood

150